Contents

What was it like for children living in Victorian Britain?

Who were the Victorians and when did they live?   4

What was life like for a poor child in the 1840s?   10

Who helped to improve the lives of Victorian children?   14

What was it like going to school at the end of the 19th century? 16

How did different Victorian children use their spare time?   20

How did life change for children living in Victorian Britain?   24

How did life change in our locality in Victorian times?   26

Finding the evidence   28

Timeline   30

See for yourself   30

Glossary   31

Index   32

What do the symbols mean?

The following symbols are used throughout the book:

 Source

 Word detective

 Biography

 See for yourself

Who were the Victorians and when did they live?

The Victorians were the people who lived in Britain during the time of Queen Victoria. She was queen for over 63 years, from 1837 to 1901. During her **reign**, Britain became the richest and most powerful nation in the world. This was a time of reform, or change. More children went to school instead of going to work. Mines and **factories** became safer, and the streets and drinking water became cleaner.

The royal family

Queen Victoria married Prince Albert in 1840. They had nine children: four sons and five daughters. The children were looked after by servants a lot of the time, but Victoria and Albert enjoyed relaxing with them when they could. Albert took charge of their education. Tutors gave them daily lessons in the schoolroom. The prince himself took them on nature walks.

This photograph of the royal family was taken in 1857 at Osborne House, their home on the Isle of Wight. Photography had been invented in 1839. Victoria is sitting, with her youngest daughter, Beatrice, on her lap.

The queen was determined that the royal children should not be spoiled. Their food was simple and their clothes were handed down to each other. Vicky, the eldest daughter, was very clever. By the age of three, she could speak French, German, and English well.

VICTORIAN BRITAIN

JANE SHUTER

www.heinemann.co.uk/library
Visit our website to find out more information about **Heinemann Library** books.

To order:
☎ Phone 44 (0) 1865 888066
▤ Send a fax to 44 (0) 1865 314091
▢ Visit the Heinemann Bookshop at www.heinemann.co.uk/library to browse our catalogue and order online.

First published in Great Britain by Heinemann Library, Halley Court, Jordan Hill, Oxford OX2 8EJ, part of Harcourt Education. Heinemann is a registered trademark of Harcourt Education Ltd.

Editorial: Jilly Attwood, Kathy Peltan and Vicki Yates
Design: Dave Poole and Tokay Interactive Ltd
Picture Research: Hannah Taylor
Production: Camilla Smith

Originated by Chroma Graphics (Overseas) Pte. Ltd
Printed in China by WKT Company Limited

ISBN 0 431 07906 4 (hardback)
10 09 08 07 06
10 9 8 7 6 5 4 3 2 1

ISBN 0 431 07912 9 (paperback)
10 09 08 07 06
10 9 8 7 6 5 4 3 2 1

British Library Cataloguing in Publication Data
Shuter, Jane
Victorian Britain
941'.081
A full catalogue record for this book is available from the British Library.

Acknowledgements
The publishers would like to thank the following for permission to reproduce photographs:
Alamy Images p. **28** (Photofusion Picture Library); Bridgeman Art Library p. **5** (Royal Holloway, University of London), **10** (British Museum); Corbis pp. **16**, **23** (Hulton-Deutsch Collection), p. **8**; Format p. **19** (Maggie Murray); Getty Images pp. **4**, **7**, **13**, **20**, **22**, **26**, **27** (Hulton Archive); Harcourt Education Ltd pp. **14**, **25t**, **25b** (Phil Bratt), **17t**, **17b** (Debbie Rowe), pp. **18**, **21**, **24**; Popperfoto p. **15**; Topham Picturepoint p. **6**, p. **12** (Fotomas); V & A Images p. **11**.

Cover photograph of a child working in a textile factory, reproduced with permission of Topham Picturepoint/Photri.

The publishers would like to thank Robyn Hardyman, Bob Rees and Caroline Landon for their assistance in the preparation of this book.

Every effort has been made to contact copyright holders of any material reproduced in this book. Any omissions will be rectified in subsequent printings if notice is given to the publishers.

Any words appearing in the text in bold, **like this**, are explained in the glossary.

Queen Victoria

Victoria (1819–1901) was born in May 1819. She became queen in June 1837, when she was eighteen years old. In 1861, Victoria's husband Albert died of **typhoid**. Victoria was very upset, and she stopped going out in public. This made her less popular, but she still carried on ruling as queen until she died in 1901. She **reigned** longer than any other British monarch.

The class system

Victorian society had different classes of people. A person's class showed in everything they did: their work, their home, even the things they did for fun. Upper class people were very rich and did not have to work. They lived in large houses, with lots of servants. Nannies looked after the children.

Middle class people worked in jobs, such as doctors and lawyers. They lived in quite big houses and had a few servants. The men worked and the women stayed at home.

Exploring further

The Heinemann Explore website and CD-ROM includes text on all the key topics about the Victorians. You can explore pictures, biographies, written sources, and lots of activities. Go to the Contents screen. Click on the blue words in the list and off you go!

Working class people had to work very hard. Sometimes their home came with the father's job; if he lost his job, the family lost their home. Everyone had to work, even the children.

After the working class came the poor. They had to do the jobs nobody else wanted to, just to get some money. Many could not find work at all.

These poor families, painted in 1874, have no homes. They are waiting to go into the **workhouse**, where they will be split up and given work.

Family life

In 1870 the average family had five or six children. The father was the head of the household, and had to be obeyed. In middle class families, the children spent most of the day in the nursery, with a nanny. In the evenings, the family would spend time together, playing the piano, reading aloud, or playing games such as cards or chess.

When they grew up, the sons were expected to work in jobs similar to their father's. The girls were expected to marry a man from the middle or upper class.

Margaret Cunningham wrote this about her middle class upbringing as the daughter of a vicar.

We were looked after by a governess, Miss Tait. We had lessons all morning, lunch with our parents (rather nerve-racking, as Miss Tait was watching our behaviour closely) and then walks in the afternoon. After schoolroom tea, we went down to the drawing room for an hour with our mother ... She played with us, games like Tippit and Hunt the Thimble. Then she would read us a story.

The Victorians were great believers in family life. This middle class family are spending time together singing and playing the piano.

Servants

Most middle and upper class households had servants to do the daily work. Servants lived in the house. All servants were working class, but some jobs were more important than others. The most important indoor servant was the butler. He organized all of the other servants. The cook was the most important of the kitchen staff. She was helped by other servants. The least important servant was the scullery maid, who cleaned up in the kitchen.

Exploring further

Use the Heinemann Explore CD-ROM or website to find out more about:

- a typical meal for a middle class family
- the clothes worn by children and servants.

Look in 'Written Sources'.

Rich people needed lots of servants to run their large homes. Each servant had clearly defined jobs to do. The head of the family often had the servants photographed in a group like this. This picture was taken in 1885.

The growth of industry

In Victorian times, the introduction of steam-powered machines made Britain the first ever **industrialized** nation. From the late 1830s until the 1870s, Britain made most of the world's goods, such as cloth made from cotton. Many factories were built, so goods could be made quickly and cheaply. British goods were cheap and sold very well. Victorian Britain grew very rich and powerful.

In 1851, the Great Exhibition was organized in London, to celebrate 'the industry of all nations'. The nation with the most exhibits was, of course, Britain. The Crystal Palace was built to house the exhibition. It was made of iron and glass, and covered an area the size of four football pitches.

Towns

The new factories needed more people to work in them, so many towns grew rapidly. In 1801 the population of Leeds was 53,000. By 1851, it had grown to 172,000. By 1901, it was 429,000. The new houses built for the workers were crowded and unhealthy.

The British Empire

The **British Empire** became large during Victoria's reign. The army spent a lot of time looking after the other **colonies** in the empire, and new land was taken over for the empire. Better transport and communications helped Britain build its empire.

Britain wanted to take over more colonies so it could be more powerful. Building an empire like this helped British trade. Britain had land in Africa, India, and Asia. These places had to sell goods to Britain and Europe, and to buy British goods. This made Britain very rich.

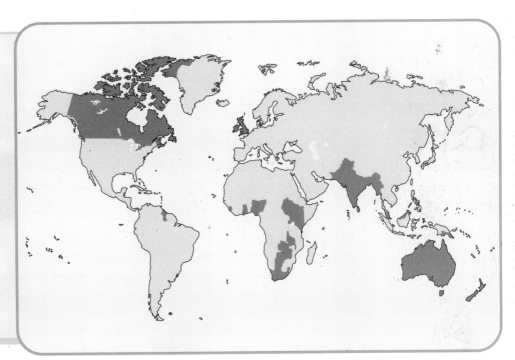

At its height in 1899, the British Empire covered one-fifth of the Earth's land surface, and contained over 370 million people. The land marked in orange on the map was all part of the British Empire.

Government help

In early Victorian times, the **government** did not think it was their job to help improve the living and working conditions of the poor. However, gradually they did start to try to make people's lives better. They passed laws that made life safer and easier for people at work. They also passed laws to make children spend more time at school.

What was life like for a poor child in the 1840s?

Life was hard for poor children living in the 1840s. Their homes were small and cold. Many began working when they were only six years old because their families needed the money to buy food. This meant they did not go to school. They worked long hours in **factories**, mines, and farms. These places were dirty and unsafe for children.

A farm worker remembers his boyhood in the mid 1800s.

'I started work scaring birds when I was six or seven years old. I worked all the time it was light, up to twelve hours each day in the summer. If I fell asleep, the farmer would whip me as punishment,'

Country life

Most people in the country worked on the big **estates** owned by the rich. Farmworkers' children worked too. Older boys helped with the heavy work, like ploughing and harvesting. Girls helped in the house and **dairy**, and looked after the animals.

The homes of poor children were small, cold and crowded. The children had very little time to play. They ate mostly bread and vegetables. Poor people could not afford to buy meat, but ate wild animals, like rabbits. If their parents could afford to keep a cow or some chickens, they would have eggs and milk as well.

This painting shows a young girl in Victorian times working on a farm. She is plucking the feathers from a chicken.

Nowhere to live

Poor children who lived in cities had very hard lives. Some of the poorest children had no homes, and often no food. They had to beg or steal to get what they needed. If they were found in the streets by the police, they were put in an **orphanage**. The children there were given very little food, and were sent out to do dirty jobs, such as sweeping chimneys.

Poor health

In the 1840s, a lot of poor children did not live very long. Living and working in such terrible conditions was so hard that many fell ill and died.

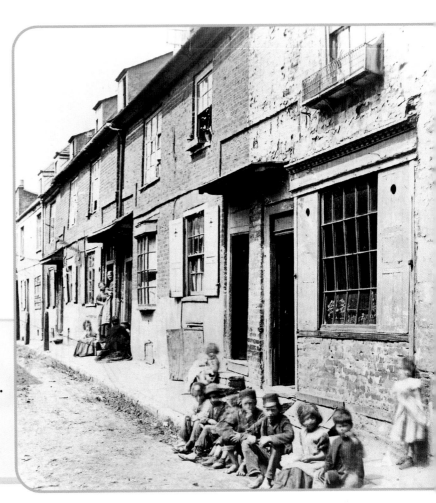

These run-down houses in London were home to the children you see in the picture. Life certainly would not have been comfortable for these children.

This is part of the **census** report for 1851.

Working class children work from an early age. Even the lowest wages paid to such a child are such a help to their parents that the temptation to keep them away from school is too great to be resisted. Many children find permanent work as early as the age of nine. In towns employment begins even earlier. Children work at needle making, button making, as errand boys, and in other such jobs as early as six; certainly between the ages of six and ten.

11

Children at work

In 1841, a survey found that over 970,000 children were being forced to work for their living, either in farms, **factories** and coal mines, or as servants.

Working in factories

The cloth-making factories needed lots of workers. Factory owners liked to employ children because they could pay them less than adults. They were also small enough to crawl under the machines to mend broken threads. Children worked long hours in hot, dusty rooms. They were often injured.

By 1840, laws had been passed to limit the age at which children could start work in factories, but factory owners often ignored these laws. These children are working in a cotton mill.

 This man, talking to investigators in 1832, could not find a job. His children were the only workers in the family.

*When the **mill** is busy, my wife gets them up at 2 in the morning and they are seldom in bed before 11 at night. The rest of the time they work from 6 in the morning until half past 8 at night. They are so tired by all this work that they fall asleep with their supper in their mouths. My eldest had her finger caught in a cog and screwed off below the knuckle. Because of this her wages were stopped.*

Working in mines

In 1840 many young children worked in mines. These produced the coal that drove the steam-powered machines in factories. The youngest opened the **trap** doors for the coal carts. Older children pulled the carts.

Children in coal mines worked long hours underground, in almost total darkness.

Charles Dickens

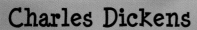

Charles Dickens (1812–1870) was a famous Victorian writer. He was born into a poor family. As a child, he worked in a factory to earn money for his family. As an adult, he began to write stories. These were published in magazines in monthly parts. Some of the most well known are *Oliver Twist*, *Nicholas Nickleby*, and *A Christmas Carol*. Dickens wrote about the problems of poverty that he saw around him. In 1858, Dickens began to read his stories to people. Many people came to hear him. Dickens died suddenly in 1870.

Exploring further

Use the Heinemann Explore CD-ROM or website to find out more about:

- a typical day for a teenage girl working in a cotton mill, in the Activity 'Working in a Factory'.

- the rules in a Manchester cotton factory in 1844. Look in 'Written Sources'.

- workhouses and orphanages. Look in 'Digging Deeper, Victorian Children'.

Who helped to improve the lives of Victorian children?

In Victorian times, some people tried to improve the lives of poor children. The **government** passed laws to improve **factories**, shorten working hours, and house the homeless. Ordinary people also helped. Some formed groups to give the poor food, clothing, and shelter. Other more powerful individuals set an example by improving the lives of the children who worked in their factories.

Model housing

Robert Owen was a factory owner from New Lanark, in Scotland. He saw that people worked better if they were happy and well. He built houses for his workers, paid them well, and did not let them work long hours.

In 1850, **mill** owner Sir Titus Salt moved his works from crowded Bradford into the open countryside and founded Saltaire. There he built a modern mill and surrounded it with about 850 houses for his workers. Other owners followed Salt's example. In 1888, soap manufacturer William Lever built Port Sunlight in Merseyside. In 1893, George Cadbury founded the 'model village' of Bournville, near Birmingham, for the workers in his chocolate factory.

William Lever wanted his workers to share in his wealth, which they had helped to create. The houses in Port Sunlight were comfortable and **hygienic**. The village also provided schools, libraries, and other facilities for people to improve themselves through learning.

Changes to the law

Eventually, new laws were passed. These laws cut down the time that children could work in factories and mines, and stopped very young children from working at all. New **inspectors** were sent out to see if the owners were obeying the law. Over the years, work for children became much better.

Lord Shaftesbury was a member of **Parliament** who pushed hard to get laws passed to improve working life in factories and mines. Here we can see him visiting a ragged school which was set up to give an education to the very poorest children. If this school had not existed, these children would probably have been out at work, maybe in a factory or in a mine.

These were the most important changes in the law:

1833 Factory Act	Starting age = 9 years. Hours: ages 9–13 = 9; ages 13–16 = 12; no night work for those under 18 years.
1844 Factory Act	Hours: ages 9–13 = 6.5; ages 13–18 = 12; dangerous machinery to be fenced in.
1847 Factory Act	Hours: ages 9–18 = 10, night and day.
1860 Mines Act	Starting age for underground work = 12; safety measures improved.
1867 Factory Act	All factory workers could only work 10 hours a day.

Dr Barnardo

Thomas John Barnardo (1845–1905) was born in Dublin, Ireland. In 1866 he moved to London. He worked in local **ragged schools** and in the **slums**. He decided to try to help the many homeless people. In 1870, Barnardo set up his first home for boys. It provided food and a roof over their heads. He was helped by Lord Shaftesbury. In 1874, Barnardo also set up a home for girls. In Dr Barnardo's homes, children were able to learn skills that would help them find a job and bring in money. By the time he died in 1905, Barnardo had helped thousands of children.

What was it like going to school at the end of the 19th century?

There were many schools in Victorian times. The rich and the middle classes paid for their children to go to private schools. Some of the poorest children went to **ragged schools**. From 1880, all children aged between five and ten had to go to school, but most still had to pay for it. In 1891, a law was passed to give free education to all children aged five to thirteen.

Ragged schools

Ragged schools were set up from 1840 onwards to provide free education for the poorest children, aged five to ten.

Board schools

New government **board schools** were set up all over the country. These had an infants' school for boys and girls aged three to seven, and separate boys' and girls' schools for the older children. Children over seven years old were divided into levels called standards. To move up to the next standard, they had to pass a test. There were up to 70 children in each class.

In Victorian schools, boys and girls were often taught in separate classes. The children sat at desks in rows. There were only a few pictures on the walls.

See for yourself

Ragged School Museum, East London

In 1876, Dr Barnardo started a ragged school in a converted warehouse in East London. It provided children aged between five and ten with lessons, meals and help with finding a job. By 1879 it was the largest of the 144 ragged schools in London. In 1895 it expanded into the warehouse next door. By 1896, there were 1075 children attending the day schools and 2460 attending the Sunday school.

PE lessons were called drill. The children were made to jump, bend, and march up and down in the playground like soldiers.

The school day

The school day began at 9 a.m. The children's names were read out, then the teachers looked to see if any of the children were dirty or ill. Dirty children were sent to the toilets to wash.

Morning lessons were reading, writing, and maths. Younger children had to say or copy out letters. Older children might write down a passage read out by the teacher. The children had to be good and quiet. If they were naughty, they were hit with a stick.

In the afternoon, the girls had sewing lessons and the boys had art lessons. Lessons ended at 3.45 p.m. The books and ink pots were given in, and the children said their prayers. At 4 p.m. they had to march out of the classroom.

Leaving school

Children had to stay in school until they passed a test when they were thirteen years old. School **inspectors** gave the tests, and schools were given money for each child who passed. The teachers knew what would be in the tests and made sure the children knew the answers, so they would pass. This meant the school would get more money.

This report was written by a school inspector in 1869

It is possible to get children through the reading, writing, and maths exam without their knowing how to read, write, or do mathematics. A book is chosen at the beginning of the year for each standard, all year the children read this book, over and over. When the inspector comes they can read a sentence or two from this book; but cannot read any other book fluently.

Exploring further

Use the Heinemann Explore CD-ROM or website to find out more about:

- the school life of a boy called William Webb, described in 1880. Look in 'Written Sources'.

- how new laws affected children's experiences of school, in the Activity 'Schools in Victorian times'.

Young children wrote on a slate with a pencil. The older children wrote on paper with a wooden pen which they dipped into a pot of ink.

How did different Victorian children use their spare time?

Children used their spare time differently, depending on their social class.

Poor children

Poor children had little spare time, as they were often at work. When they did play, they often played games outside in the streets or fields, in large groups.

These children are dancing around a lamp-post. Children had to make up their own games. There was no television or radio, and no computer games.

Upper class and middle class children

Boys from rich families played with balls, drums, boats, bricks, marbles, toy trains, and toy soldiers. Girls played with dolls, dolls' houses, teasets, and sewing kits. They only had a few books to read.

This set of dressing-up dolls would have belonged to a girl from the middle or upper class.

Sundays

Most children had some spare time on Sundays. They wore their Sunday best clothes and were expected to go to church. However, they were not allowed to play noisy games. They played quietly with toys such as a Noah's ark. They also read the Bible.

Exploring further

Use the Heinemann Explore CD-ROM or website to find out more about typical Victorian toys and games in the Activity 'Playtime'.

Public places

The Victorians believed it was important for people to behave well at all times, and to try and improve themselves through learning. They built many public museums and libraries. Entry to these was free. Anyone could go and look at works of art and other objects of interest or read books, in their spare time. They also encouraged people to go to public parks and gardens to keep healthy.

A family celebrate Christmas at home. Many of our Christmas traditions began in Victorian times, such as Christmas fir trees, carol singing, decorating with holly and ivy, and Christmas cards.

Days out

In 1871, the government introduced bank holidays – a few Mondays during the year when all banks, factories, shops, and offices were closed. Families looked for ways to spend this time. Rail travel meant people could travel further, faster, and more cheaply than before. Short trips to the countryside or seaside became popular. Other family outings might be to the circus or theatre, the funfair, the zoo, or a museum.

Holidays

It was not until the 1890s that family holidays became more common. Workers probably had a week's holiday every year. Some stayed at home, others went to the seaside. Poorer people went on working holidays. For example, families from London's East End went to Kent to pick fruit and **hops** on farms.

Thomas Cook

Thomas Cook was one of the first people to offer organized railway trips. Many working people went on his trips to the Great Exhibition in 1851; they also went to the seaside. Cook also organized more expensive trips abroad for the upper classes. France, Italy, and Switzerland were popular destinations. Even on holiday the rich kept themselves apart from middle class and working class people.

This Manchester woman is remembering her childhood in the 1890s.

*Once a year, during **wakes week**, the **mills** all closed down ... So you went off to Blackpool with all your neighbours and were never lonely. You took the same lodgings year after year in the same place, and spent a year's savings on a glorious spree.*

Hastings, in East Sussex, was a popular seaside resort by 1890. It had big hotels on the seafront. It also had bathing machines on wheels for people to change in and swim from. Other popular coastal towns were Blackpool, Southend, Morecambe, and Brighton.

Isambard Kingdom Brunel

Isambard Kingdom Brunel (1806–1859) was a railway **engineer**. He was behind the building of the Great Western Railway, which first ran from Paddington Station in London to Bristol and opened in 1841. Railway lines like these made short holidays and trips possible. Brunel also built huge steamships to carry passengers from Bristol across the Atlantic Ocean. The *Great Eastern* steamship (built in 1858) could carry 4000 passengers. Brunel worked so hard, it made him ill. He died when he was only in his fifties.

How did life change for children living in Victorian Britain?

In Victorian times, life changed less for upper class children than it did for working class children. The rich were still educated and did not need to work when they grew up.

New laws

A lot of things changed for poor children between 1837 and 1901. New laws meant that they did not have to start work so young. When they did go to work, they did not have to work such long hours. Instead of working, poor children could go to school.

New inventions

Life also changed for middle class children. New inventions, such as the telephone and the typewriter, created new jobs for them when they grew up. Girls could find more work, so they did not have to marry to leave home.

Cities had certainly changed by 1900, when this photograph of central London was taken. Roads were paved, and there were pavements and streetlights. Buses, trams, and bicycles were new forms of transport.

These figures show how the average weights of factory children (in lbs) increased between 1833 (when the first Factory Act was passed) and 1873.

Age last birthday	9	10	11	12
weight in 1833 (lb)	52	57	62	66
weight in 1873 (lb)	59	62	67	70

Public health

By the 1850s, the **government** understood that dirt could make you ill. They began to make laws about public health. Drains were built, rubbish was collected, and people were able to drink clean water. By the end of Victorian times, fewer people were dying from diseases. Children were healthier and lived longer.

See for yourself

Saltaire Village, Bradford

Saltaire is a village built by Sir Titus Salt for the workers in his woollen **mill**. There are about 850 houses in 22 streets, as well as a school, a hospital, a fire station, churches, a park, wash-houses, and a railway station. Most of the village remains as it was when Salt died in 1876.

Salt was one of the factory owners who believed that they should improve the living and working conditions of their workers. They also believed that happier and healthier workers would work harder, and so be good for their businesses.

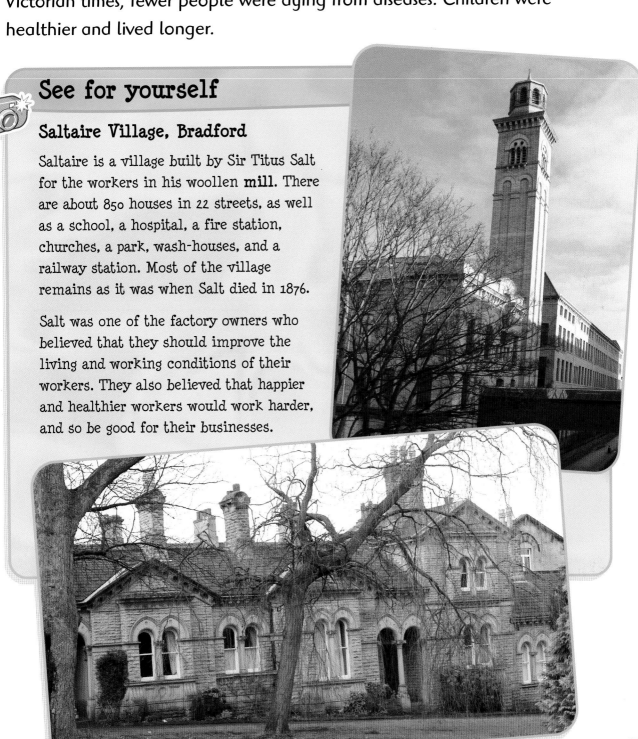

Industry and towns

In 1801, almost 70 per cent of the population of Britain lived in the countryside. By 1901, it was only 30 per cent. Millions of people had moved to the towns to look for work. In the middle of the town were the **factories**. Houses for the workers were built around them. Shops and pubs were built near by. By 1851, ten cities, including Manchester, Liverpool and Glasgow, had more than 100,000 inhabitants. Biggest of all was London, with nearly 2,500,000.

In this industrial town of the 1850s, the houses and factory buildings are crammed close together. The chimneys belch out smoke, filling the air with dust and soot.

Transport

The railways were very important for the growth of industry. Trains carried goods around the country, including coal from the mines of Wales and northern England to factories, iron **foundries,** and gasworks. Railways changed the landscape. Tunnels, cuttings, and bridges were made. New lines cut across towns on their way to new stations.

The new steamships could **import** goods from other countries. New foods began to come into Britain. As food became easier to transport, it also became cheaper to buy.

Exploring further

Use the Heinemann Explore CD-ROM or website to find out more about an early steam engine in action, in a video clip. Look in 'Media Bank'.

Buildings

Our villages, towns, and cities are full of Victorian buildings. Many schools were built, as new laws made more children go to school. New churches encouraged more people to worship regularly and lead good Christian lives. Museums and libraries were built so that people could improve themselves by learning.

Victorian buildings were often built of red brick or stone. Public buildings were grand and ornately decorated. Houses were roofed with slate tiles and had a chimney.

Word detective

There is evidence of Victorian times in the street names of our towns and cities. Many streets were named after Victoria, Albert, and their children. Others were named after places in the **British Empire** or after famous battle victories.

The Victorians built many terraces of brick houses like these to house factory workers.

Finding the evidence

There will have been many changes in your area during Victorian times, and you can see evidence of those changes today. There are many kinds of evidence you can use to find out about the changes.

Public records

Libraries, local museums, and parish churches have records and collections from Victorian times. Libraries and museums may have photographs and maps of your area, that show how it has changed, as well as newspapers, letters, and objects from the past. Churches keep records of births, christenings, marriages, and burials. Gravestones can also tell you how long people lived. County Record Offices keep **census** material and other local records.

Buildings

Look for public buildings built by the Victorians, such as town halls, museums, libraries, churches, schools, and railway stations. Look for private buildings too. As towns grew, the Victorians built many new houses for the workers. Richer people built big houses on the edges of towns and in the country.

A network of railways spread across Britain in the 1840s. St Pancras station, in London, was a particularly grand Victorian railway station. It was built for the Midland Railway in 1868. It took 6000 men four years to build it.

Who lived and worked here in Victorian times?

To find out who lived in your area in 1841 and in 1891, look at the **census**. You can find the census at your County Record Office. A census is a list that shows who lives in every house in the country. It also lists their names and ages, where they were born, and what work they do.

The first census was in 1801. Since then, there has been a census every ten years. The results from each census are kept secret for 100 years. You can now look at the census information taken during Victorian times.

What will the census tell me?

A census from your area will tell you how big the families were and what work people did. For example, it will show that in 1891 there were fewer children working than there had been in 1841, because in 1891 they had to go to school.

The information in a census may not be completely accurate. Census takers sometimes made mistakes, or made up information to save time. Sometimes people did not tell them the truth. However, the information is still accurate enough to be useful.

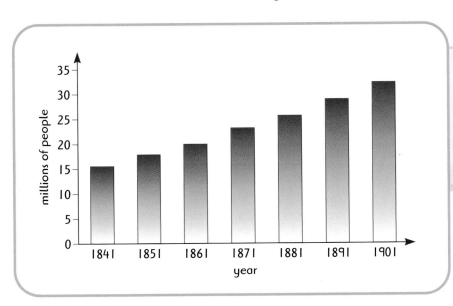

This bar graph shows the population figures taken from censuses in Britain between 1841 and 1901.

Timeline

1819	Victoria is born
1837	Victoria becomes queen, aged eighteen
1840	Victoria marries her cousin, Albert
	The first **ragged schools** are set up
1851	The **census** lists people's occupations for the first time
	The Great Exhibition takes places in London
1861	Prince Albert dies of **typhoid**
1863	The first underground railway line opens in London
1867	A new law states that all **factory** workers can only work ten hours a day
1870	Dr Barnardo opens his first home for boys
	Charles Dickens dies
1880	A new law states that children aged five to ten must go to school
1888	William Lever builds Port Sunlight, in Merseyside, for his factory workers
1891	All children aged five to thirteen can receive free schooling
1901	Queen Victoria dies. Her son Edward becomes King Edward VII.

See for yourself

Blists Hill Victorian town, Shropshire
At this open-air museum a small Victorian town has been created on the banks of the Shropshire canal.

Didcot Railway Centre, Didcot, Oxfordshire
Steam engines and other railway exhibits from the Great Western Railway can be explored here.

Museum of Childhood, Edinburgh
The museum has many Victorian toys and games.

National Railway Museum, York
You can see a large collection of old steam engines and other railway exhibits here.

Natural History Museum, London
This amazing building is typical of the Victorians' love of grand public projects. It houses the national collection of natural history.

New Lanark Visitor Centre, New Lanark, Scotland
Robert Owen's cotton **mill** village has been restored for visitors.

Port Sunlight, Merseyside
You can visit the model village built by Lord Lever for his workers.

Ragged School Museum, Copperfield Road, East London
In a re-created classroom of the period, visitors can experience how Victorian children were taught. There are also displays on local history.

SS *Great Britain*, Bristol
The great steamship built by Brunel is undergoing restoration in the dock where she was built.

Salts Mill and Saltaire, Shipley, Bradford
Visit the mill and the model village built by Sir Titus Salt for his workers.

Glossary

board school school set up by a Board of Education using money given by the government

British Empire lands that Britain controlled all over the world

census count of all the people in every home in the country on a particular day

colony land in which people from a foreign country settle and that is ruled from a distance by that country

dairy place on a farm where milk was stored and where butter and cheese were made

engineer person trained in designing, constructing, and maintaining machinery, bridges, and so on

estate area of land owned by one person or family

factory short for 'manufactory', a place where lots of workers and machines make large amounts of the same thing (e.g. cloth)

foundry place where iron is melted, refined, and cast

government people who run a country

hops plant whose flowers are dried and used in brewing beer and in medicines

hygiene cleanliness needed to keep healthy

import to bring in goods, such as food, from another country

industrialized where heavy mechanized or factory industries, such as mining or cloth-making, have been widely developed

inspector person who is given the job of going to a factory, school, or other place to make sure that the people there are obeying the laws made about work, education, etc.

mill factory that makes cloth

orphanage place where a child whose parents have both died is sent to live

Parliament the House of Lords (nobles and important churchmen) and the House of Commons (elected members – MPs) who meet to advise the monarch

ragged school school set up specially to teach poor children

reign length of time a king or queen rules a country

slum poorest, most overcrowded, and uncared for part of a town or city

trap wooden door opened and closed to allow fresh air into mines

typhoid infection by bacteria transmitted in unclean water or food

wakes week annual week's holiday given to factory workers in summer

workhouse place set up by the government where poor people with no money could go and be given a bed, food, and work

Index

Albert, Prince 4, 5

bank holidays 22
Barnardo, Dr Thomas John 15, 17
Board schools 16
Bournville 14
British Empire 9
Brunel, Isambard Kingdom 23

Cadbury, George 14
census 11, 28, 29
child workers 10, 11, 12–13, 15, 24
children 4, 6, 9, 10–21, 24, 25, 27
Christmas traditions 22
church attendance 21, 27
church records 28
class system 5
coal mines 4, 10, 12, 13, 15, 26
Cook, Thomas 23
countryside 10, 27

Dickens, Charles 13
diseases 5, 25

engineering 23

factories 4, 8, 10, 12, 14, 15, 26
Factory Acts 15, 24
factory inspectors 15
family life 6
farming 10, 12
food 10, 27

games 6, 20
governesses and tutors 4, 6
government 9, 14, 22, 25
Great Exhibition 8, 23

health 11, 21, 25
holidays 22, 23
homeless people 5, 11, 14, 15
housing 10, 11, 14, 26, 27, 28

industry 8, 26
inventions 4, 24

laws 9, 12, 14, 15, 16, 24
Lever, William 14
libraries and museums 14, 21, 22, 26, 28

middle class people 5, 6, 7, 16, 20, 23, 24
mills 12, 14, 23

orphanages 11
Osborne House 4
Owen, Robert 14

PE lessons 18
photography 4
poor people 5, 9, 10–15, 20
population 8, 26, 29
Port Sunlight 14
public buildings 27, 28
public records 26, 29
punishment 10, 18

ragged schools 15, 16, 17
rail travel 22, 23, 26, 28
rich people 5, 7, 10, 16, 20, 23, 28

St Pancras station 28
Salt, Sir Titus 14, 25
Saltaire 14, 25
school inspectors 19
schools 4, 9, 15, 16–19, 27

seaside resorts 23
servants 4, 5, 7, 12
Shaftesbury, Lord 15
slums 15
spare time 6, 20–3
steamships 23, 26
street names 27
Sunday schools 17
Sundays 21

towns, industrial 8, 26
toys 20, 21
transport 9, 22, 23, 24, 26
typhoid 5

upper class people 5, 7, 20, 23, 24

Victoria, Queen 4, 5

Wakes Week 23
work 5, 6, 10, 11, 12–13, 14, 15, 24, 25
workhouses 5
working class people 5, 11, 22, 23, 24

Titles in the *New Explore History* series include:

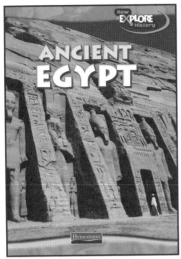

Hardback   0 431 07902 1

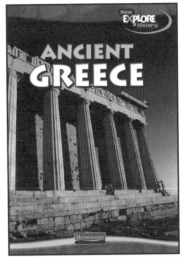

Hardback   0 431 07905 6

Hardback   0 431 07907 2

Hardback   0 431 07903 X

Hardback   0 431 07904 8

Hardback   0 431 07906 4

Find out about other titles from Heinemann Library on our website www.heinemann.co.uk/library